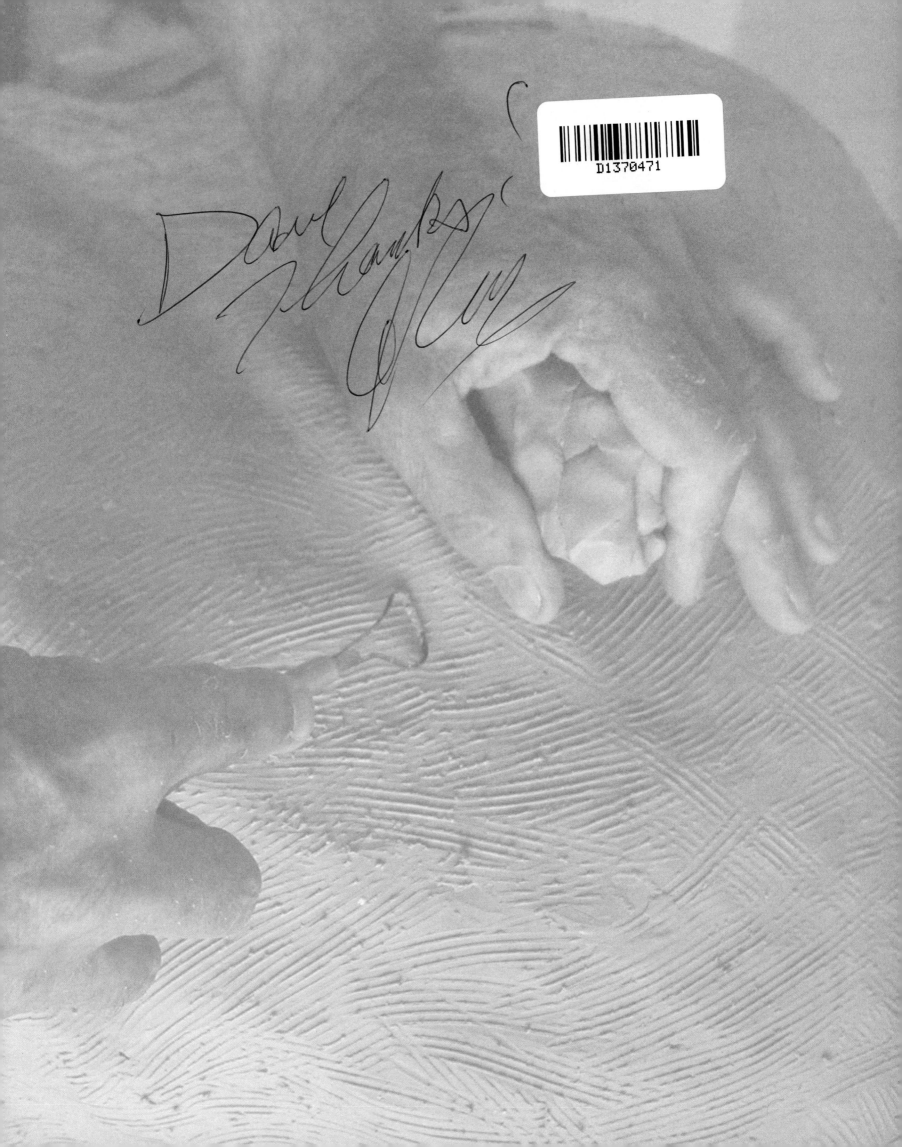

THE ART
of
Arthur H. Norby

A C K N O W L E D G M E N T S

I know I am a very lucky man. I recognized early that to seek fame and fortune as an artist is the height of foolhardiness. Instead, I have sought only to enjoy my life as an artist while attempting to create works which will justify spending a life.

In spite of sometimes flowery rhetoric, I have only tried to give in to my curiosity, to create works whose quality will not embarrass my heirs, and to occasionally surprise myself when I reach just a little beyond my expectations. This book would not have been possible without the help of some very important people whom I would like to thank.

Of course, thanks to the several hundred collectors who have allowed me to grow as an artist. Most notable, in the earlier years was "Doc" Munneke who was my first major collector. Also, thanks to Donn Lorenz, whose belief in me helped me through some major transitions. Bob, Mary, Woody and Jonette will know why I thank them.

My children and their mother may not realize how important their love and understanding have always been, as has been the moral support of my extended family, and I wish to thank them.

My editor, Sherry Weinstein, can never be repaid for the grueling task she performed, nor can I thank the publisher, Dennis Kirk, to the degree he deserves.

Last, first and most, however, I want to thank my wife, Kathryn, for not only her love and support in this project, but for her bulldog tenacity in seeing that all my thoughts made it through the computer processes, and for buoying me up in those moments when I really needed her support.

Copyright © 2002 Arthur H. Norby
All works of art copyright © Arthur H. Norby

Produced by:
Dennis Kirk/International Graphics
Scottsdale, Arizona 85259

Photo Credits:
Jack Elness
George Heinrich
Rose Lausten
Michael Slack
Kathryn Spangler-Norby

Standard Edition: ISBN 1-889741-55-8
Limited Edition: ISBN 1-889741-56-8

Printed in Singapore

TABLE OF CONTENTS

ARTIST'S STATEMENT

"It is never my intention to create scale models of things, but rather to create my impression of the model's essence as in one deep breath held forever. My subjects are as varied as my method of depicting them. Sometimes my sculpture is smooth and slick, and at other times records only raw impressions. Sharing my sculpture is a way to share my view of life."

Looking Within...

By and large, life is made-up of small defining moments. Yet, after working for more than twenty-five years as an artist, I cannot identify the exact point in time or single event that caused me to take this path, for there were many. And there may well be more, which I have yet to discover. Some of those with whom I grew up seemed to know from childhood the route that would be theirs, but I was nearly forty before I found mine, and am pleased to still be on a journey of self-discovery.

On the evening of Christmas Day, 1937, I was born in the small town of Montevideo, Minnesota. Until I reached my teens, I believed my hometown to be a great metropolis and influential center of the world. Later, as a young man who thought he knew it all, I began to reject those early perceptions. Today, as a mature adult, I am proud to admit that the place of my birth was—and to this day remains—the influential center of my world. Although my parents and grandparents were poor beyond my understanding, I was raised with the kind of personal wealth that lasts a lifetime, despite any lack of material goods. In retrospect, it seems that such hardship describes most of rural America in the years between the Great Depression and World War II.

At the age of four my art career began taking shape, literally, in the form of the Gibson Girls, who had been the rage in advertising for several decades. With jars of used pencils and crayons—along with an abundance of patience—my aunts taught me to sketch the glamorous women, and went on to show me how to draw squares that would magically become three-dimensional boxes with the addition of just a couple of lines. As most little boys would, I found the 3-D geometric shapes far more exciting than the feminine ones. Apparently, I still had much to learn.

In the fifth grade I had my first real run-in with the educational system and its relationship to art. My class was assigned to draw a barn with its doors, windows and boards, and to color the barn. Of course, all the barns were red, but of the entire class only my barn had the boards going up and down. After a short but heated discussion, my drawing was pulled out of my hands, crumpled up, and thrown in the wastebasket by my teacher. Within her frame of reference, all siding on buildings had to be horizontal, which made mine wrong. Too bad she had never seen my grandparents' barn, on which the siding ran vertically.

Left: "Trail to Fort Bowie"
Oil on Canvas

"VOYAGER"

The Minnesota Heritage Collection; I particularly like the "Voyager" as it was the first time I combined subjects from two different scales.

The Statue that Would Impact My Life...

People laugh nervously when I tell them I failed art in the seventh grade. This is one academic failure that I do not blame on the teacher or the system. During this immature and irresponsible stage, I simply did not understand the value of completing assigned tasks, especially when I viewed such assignments as tedious repetition.

While I was busy challenging the educational system, failing art, and feeling like I was in the wrong place at the wrong time, Montevideo was named the sister city to Montevideo, Uruguay. The attention and festivities focused on my hometown did much to confirm my prior notion that it was, in fact, the center of the universe, and I began to feel like I was once again part of something great. At the age of twelve I stood proudly on the street with my grandfather and watched as a thirteen-foot bronze sculpture of Jose Artigas—Argentina's counterpart to George Washington—was unloaded and set in place. I would not recognize the full impact of that "defining moment" for almost thirty years, finally becoming aware that this event had actually inspired me, early on, to be a sculptor.

Moving Out and Moving On...

In the early fifties my family was caught in the turmoil of the Korean War. Forfeiting the safety of life in small town America, we moved to Denver, where my father made rockets for the war effort. Returning to Minnesota in 1954, I realized that Denver had colored my thinking, forever. When I graduated from high school in 1955—certain that I knew, if not everything, at least more than my parents did—I promptly left home for Denver. Soon, I joined the Navy, where I spent the next ten years on active service, followed by another decade in the Naval Reserve.

With a starter set of oils and a "how to" book, I created my first "grown-up" painting in 1961. Creating art was a new-found passion for me, but because we were so poor I had to resort to painting on old window shades because there was no money for canvas. As desperate as I was for money in the early sixties, I turned down $150 for an oil painting of a moose, done on illustration board. Even though I didn't know anyone who had ever sold a painting, I believed mine was worth more than I had been offered. Several months later I spilled coffee on the piece and spoiled my chances of ever getting a higher bid!

While on active duty, I was assigned to the Seabees and deployed to Puerto Rico, where we were building military housing. During that time I was the editor of the Battalion newspaper as well as the resident cartoonist. When my Battalion returned to the United States, I spent the remainder of my first enlistment as the illustrator, draftsman and artistic coordinator for the Navy's Antarctic Expedition, headquartered in Davisville, Rhode Island. Part of my job was to make charts and presentations, which would all become a key component of my "art" training. Although I didn't learn how to paint or sculpt on this job, I did learn to think my way through a project, becoming skilled at the value of line and composition.

During my second enlistment I attended an advanced engineering school in California and spent a number of years as an architectural and civil draftsman, and surveyor. On leaving the Navy in 1967, I went into the insurance business, selling life and health insurance in Seattle. Later, I returned to Minnesota, and although my interest in insurance had run its course within a couple of years, those years gave me the marketing and business skills I have used throughout my art career. Just as important, the engineering training I had received in the Navy gave me skills that would, in the long run, become critical to my creation of large-scale sculptures.

With providence guiding me, I became involved with the Kandiyohi County art organization, a cooperative of art teachers, artists and supporters of the arts, with which I was affiliated through the early eighties. Early on, I was chosen to be the director for Gallery 401, the art organization's volunteer coop gallery in Willmar, Minnesota. In so many ways I had, in fact, come home.

"TAURUS"
Bronze

Hallowed Halls…

At the age of 31 I decided that I needed to go to college and learn to be an artist. Two of the most frustrating years of my life were spent in the art studio and art classes, at the hands of the academics. I had never been a great student, and between the pressure of raising a family and trying to "learn how" to be an artist, my college experience was not what I had hoped it would be. Looking back on it I can see that just

when an aspiring artist needs help most, it seems the instructor is either not available or offers criticism that is anything but constructive. For instance, after weeks of "suggesting" that I paint out a particular composition or do anything but continue with it, my instructor took it upon himself to make his own alterations to my painting. When I walked into the studio about 10:00 one morning, all of the other students were busy at their easels with their backs turned towards the center of the room, which was most unusual. The instructor was sitting at his desk across the room from my easel. My canvas had been painted out with a white gesso and with the end of his paintbrush the instructor had written, "Roses are red, Violets are blue, this painting stinks and so do you." After a few short words with the instructor, I left the campus and never returned.

For some time I blamed the system because it seemed that instructors would pick one or two students whom they thought had a particular talent and would nurture only that talent. The remaining students had to succeed or fail on their own. In the end it proved to be a valuable lesson that many artists should learn; you have to take charge of your own life and your own projects. You can't rely on someone else. If you're going to learn, you can do it with astute observation and careful listening, but you can't expect someone else to "teach" you to be a painter or sculptor.

Crisis… Not Quite at Midlife

After my university experience, I threw myself into making a living for my family by traveling from resort to resort and café to café, selling sundry items on what was called a jobber's truck. Eventually this became a wholesale sporting goods truck with which I represented, among others, a hockey skate manufacturer, firearms dealer and archery manufacturer, traveling through western Minnesota, calling on clients in the sporting goods business. Heeding my well-meaning friends—who thought I had the best inventory of sporting goods in western Minnesota—I opened my own sporting goods store. A few months after signing a three-year lease, I was to discover that the highway in front of my store was going to be expanded. Effectively, this would put me out of business, which it did, and forced me to file for bankruptcy. When I was finally out of the woods on this sporting goods fiasco, I decided—on my 38th birthday—that I owed it to myself to spend one year doing whatever I had to do to be an artist. I promised my wife that if I could not generate a living income within a year, that I would put my dream of being an artist behind me, get a job and never talk about it again. This decision was one of the primary factors in the divorce that my wife and I finalized in the spring of 1979. On the positive side, I had left myself no avenues except to move forward as an artist. All of my bridges were burned behind me so that I was literally forced to be successful and had no choice but to experiment with different mediums.

The mainstay of my income for the next two years was the creation of scrimshaw, the engraving of ivory or bone, much like it had been practiced by Eskimos and sailors during the whaling era. When I began there seemed to be no other artists in Minnesota, or in the Midwest for that matter, doing scrimshaw. So I had something of a lock on the market. Although I had to educate the majority of my buyers as to what the product was and why it had any value, it wasn't long before others around the Midwest were copying this art form. In truth, it became popular all across the country, not necessarily because of my individual efforts, but because people were simply fascinated with this very romantic and historical art form.

In the final throws of my divorce in 1979, I was living temporarily in Colorado and recognized that I was on a path that was leading me right back to my starting place. Admitting to myself that I needed to be doing something that had personal value and meaning, I sat down one afternoon and wrote out the following set of goals:

"ADAM" 1996
This sculpture was lost in the fire of 1998.

My one and only personal goal was to improve my relationship with my family, for nothing was more important to me than that.

My first professional goal was to find a better way to market my artwork. I had been attending weekend art shows, driving tens of thousands of miles and being away from home and my family for two months at a time. Although I had taught myself to fabricate silver and gold jewelry into which I placed my ivory, I had reached a monetary plateau where it was becoming difficult to sustain the income that I needed to generate.

My second professional goal was to attend three watercolor workshops. I had done watercolors in 1975 and 1976, but had never pursued it because the

"THE GREEK"
Oil Pastel

art of scrimshaw was very time consuming and I had become very focused on it.

My final professional goal for now was to pursue an interest I'd had for just about a decade, which was to create one piece of sculpture that I would be willing to cast in bronze. I had hoped to reach this goal by the end of 1979.

Within a week of establishing the final goal, I returned to Minnesota, where I borrowed $10,000 from the local credit union and opened my first art gallery, in Willmar, followed by a second gallery, in Spicer, early in 1980. Fortune was smiling on me as the gallery setting did, in fact, give me a much better venue for marketing my work. Surrounded by original creations of other artists whose work I respected, I became like a moving kaleidoscope—creating, experimenting, succeeding—steadily building a client or collector base for my own work.

Over the next twenty years I owned six art galleries and helped over one hundred artists exhibit and market their art.

My second goal of attending three watercolor workshops was short-lived. Although I enjoyed the camaraderie of the first workshop, and appreciated the spontaneity that watercolor demands, I determined it was not the medium I wanted to pursue, and attended no further workshops.

In due course, the discipline with which I was most successful was sculpture. By the end of 1979, I had created not one, but ten pieces of sculpture and cast them all in bronze! From my perspective today, I'd say that no more than three or four of these pieces actually warranted bronze, but hindsight is on target far more often than foresight. From that same perspective, though, I believe that watching these sculptures materialize from within myself showed me the kind of consummate satisfaction that could always be mine from the creation of three-dimensional art. By the mid–eighties, I was no longer doing scrimshaw, and the idea of churning out watercolors had long since passed.

Narrowing the Focus...

Now that I had found my medium of choice, I'd need to determine what subject matter, or message, I could identify as my own. For some time I had recognized that I did not want to work within the restrictions of being a wildlife artist. Being true to the artist within, I needed to allow myself more creativity than that genre would allow. Having been raised around horses, and having actually raised horses myself for several years, I pondered the idea of entering the realm of western art, but soon decided that I was not a cowboy, nor conversational enough with the subject of western art or cowboying itself to create an original body of work.

Since I have always had some interest in history, be it my own family history or that of Minnesota or the Midwest—and given that I have a romantic nature—history and historical figures had a certain appeal and seemed like a reasonable hook on which to hang my hat... at least for a time. During 1980, I began a series which I call the Minnesota Heritage Collection, representing the history of the Upper Midwest, the settling of the Red River Valley, its pioneers, farmers, the spirituality of its people... the very same earthy

"TWO POTATOES"
Oil Pastel

people with whom I had grown up. This collection, which ultimately spawned eleven pieces of sculpture, was my first very successful series and the catalyst that brought me together with my earliest—and therefore my most important—collector. Lyle "Doc" Munneke, a local MD, with his friendship and patronage, gave me the moral and emotional support to keep striving for a higher level as an artist.

In 1982, my older daughter, Kari—who had been managing the Willmar gallery—decided to go back to school and continue her education. This would mean I'd have to close one gallery or hire at least one manager. After giving the matter considerable thought, I realized that in the preceding year I had created only two pieces of sculpture because all my time was being spent on the business of art rather than the art I so dearly loved to create. Reason enough to get out of the gallery business and back to my commitment to creating images.

A Life-Altering Experience…

For the next couple of years, I shared a second floor studio with three artist friends, Bob Orr, Mary Thompson, and Woodson Whiting Grove, who were art teachers as well as producing artists. Working on what must have been highly fertile ground, we seemed to energize each other, all becoming unusually productive during that time. Unfortunately, that happy era came to a crashing halt one day in 1984 when my studio mates and I hosted a four-artist exhibit to show off our most recent sculptures and paintings. During the exhibit someone managed to deface a three-quarter life-size female figure that I was showing while it was still in the clay stage. Totally devastated, I destroyed what was left of the sculpture, never to rebuild it. I had a two-hour breakdown in which I felt my life completely unravel, and determined that this setback to my artwork and my being left me no choice but to put some distance between myself and the source of my pain. With a haunting sense of aloneness I locked up my home and left for the south of Spain. Over the next three months I traveled the local areas, particularly the Costa del Sol—coast of the sun—feasting on the art to be found in countless churches and museums… becoming whole once again.

Upon my return to the United States, I took a job in Minneapolis where I spent six months as the art director for a gift manufacturer. After leaving this company, I created a small line of oak and walnut desk accessories that I marketed through gift shows in the Midwest and Florida until the fall of 1987, when I returned to Seattle, after an absence of twenty years. Returning there without any of my artwork or art supplies, I had every intention of getting a job that would allow me to enjoy my art, but not have to earn a living from the creation of my own hands. At the end of a couple of months I recognized without question that managing someone else's business was more grueling and far less satisfying than being an independent artist. Leaving what would be my last "job," I opened a small studio gallery in Pioneer Square in downtown Seattle. Smack in the heart of the art district, this was a vibrant area in the late 1980s, with weekly art walks and brisk tourist activity that brought people to my studio.

When I first returned home in 1990, I created portrait sculptures of my parents. My portraits are perhaps notorious for not idealizing my subjects and these of my parents are no different. My mother passed away within six months of her portrait. Each time I look at it I can see her age and frailty and therein her beauty. My father's eyes reflect the weariness of caring for my mother during the years of her declining health.

In 1996 Tony's Pizza initiated a nationwide in-house promotion and wanted an award which would be re-allocated for a new division each year. I was commissioned to recreate the likeness of the company's "Tony" (16"h) in the likeness of the Heisman Trophy. Tony in his chef's hat and apron is carrying a football and reaching out to block the competition. Tony was cast in bronze and I assume he is still travelling across the country!

Education on Both Sides of the Classroom...

During my Pioneer Square era, I spent a lot of time at Pratt Fine Arts Center, Seattle's foremost studio for the visual arts. Now looked to for my expertise, I taught several workshops there, but also spent two to three hours at a time, two or three times a week in Pratt's open drawing studio. With my terra cotta and stoneware clays in hand, I did rapid studies in clay as the models moved through their poses. Learning to be spontaneous in my interpretation of the figure, I began to see the human form under considerably different conditions than I had previously done. Finally receiving the best training the art world could give me, I learned to create a small figure study in five to ten minutes, a full figure study in thirty minutes, and a twenty-four to thirty-inch sculpture in three to six hours. Although these pieces were typically primitive in their finish, the spontaneity and characteristic raw emotion of the work made them very popular with my Seattle clientele.

Picking up graphite and charcoal, and leaving my prior notions of drawing and painting behind, I began to experiment with oil pastels, learning to interpret—in a new way—what my eyes told my brain it was seeing. In the late eighties I developed a style that I enjoyed very much. An art historian from North Carolina compared these pastels to be much like that of Brach, who was Picasso's contemporary. Again the work was deliberately spontaneous, meeting the goal that I had set for myself of completing an entire pastel rendering in the amount of time determined by the model. Sometimes these would be three minutes or five minutes, almost never lasting more than fifteen minutes. Fortunately for me, the spontaneity came. I found that in a three-hour session I might do twenty or thirty pastels. When I re-evaluated the renderings back in my own studio, I might find four or five that had the look and style I was trying to achieve.

After becoming active in the International Foundation for Anti-cancer Drug Discovery, better known as IFADD, I created a bronze representation of IFADD's John Kolbe Memorial Award. This enduring tribute, entitled "Fortitude: Reaching Out to Cancer Patients," acknowledges the heroism needed to fight the scourge of cancer, and was awarded in 2001 to Congressman Matt Salmon for his tireless efforts in the War on Cancer.

The Business of Art...

At one point, a couple of collectors invited me to bring these pastels to their office. I laid my works across the entire floor. After looking at the thirty or so pastels I had brought, the collectors asked, "Which ones do you think we should buy, Art?" I said, "Well, I can't tell you which ones you should own, but I can tell you the ones you should not own based on the sophistication of your own collection." Leaving twenty of the pieces, I said "I think that any of these would fit well into your collection. There is one, however, that I'm not very interested in selling." When they asked which one that was I pointed to my favorite. They responded, "Well, if we really wanted to buy that one, what would we have to pay for it?" My reply was that the other pieces were $250 each, but if they wanted the one I had chosen for myself it would be twice as much. The couple looked at each other, smiled and bellowed, "We'll take them all!"

By the spring of 1990, I had become restless once again, and had begun to miss my family and friends back in Minnesota more than I was willing to bear. Testing the waters, so to speak, I attended the Wildlife Collectors Annual Show in Minnesota and determined that people in the Midwest did, in fact, deem my work desirable. In June of 1990, I packed up and returned to Minnesota. Before leaving Seattle, though, I had lunch with a friend and gave her one of my sculptures as a parting gift. It turns out this sculpture has come back to me in every way. That friend was Kathryn Spangler, who decided to leave Seattle and join me in Minnesota six months later. We were married in 1996, on Valentine's Day.

For Art's Sake...

Returning to Willmar, Minnesota, I rented an entire vacant storefront—about 1500 square feet of retail space—and turned this into a studio and gallery. That summer I was introduced to Donn Lorenz, who became a very strong supporter and benefactor, collecting my work and helping me achieve some of my goals over the next several years.

Donn Lorenz's first commission was a one-half life-size nude figure, which I completed that summer. This was followed by life-size portrait busts of Lorenz, his wife, and their four children, all of which were cast in bronze. The following winter he commissioned me to do my first life-size nude.

For some time I had been searching for a place where I could develop my work simply for art's sake, and perhaps open a small regional school for artists. As fate would have it, Kathy and I found—on the outskirts of Granite Falls—there had been a tuberculosis sanitarium, a beautiful set of brick buildings that had gone into disrepair since the government no longer funded the hospital. That would be the ideal setting for my dream. Moving into a small brick house just a mile downstream from the sanitarium—on the Minnesota River—we would try for the next three years to acquire the sanitarium property.

During that time, we purchased what had been an automobile dealership building, on the main highway going through Granite Falls, and converted it to an art gallery, gift shop and artist's studio. We did this with the financial assistance of Donn Lorenz and a grant from the City of Granite Falls. Until 1994, we continued to host exhibits of artists from the region, jurying high end art exhibits for which we brought in artists from Minneapolis and the surrounding rural areas. In the studio I taught workshops from time to time as we continued to try to develop an art business. While there, I began to receive public art commissions and to gain recognition as a sculptor.

It soon became apparent that we were not going to be able to buy the sanitarium property. In time, though, we discovered and fell in love with a vacant church that had been built in 1885. Its owner was currently using it for storage, and we arranged to buy this property, in Afton, a small community near St. Paul, Minnesota, for about $50,000. Over the next three years, my time was divided between creating sculpture and renovating the building into a studio and home.

From Monument to Monumental Change...

While we were still in Granite Falls, I was commissioned to do my first monumental work, a sculpture of Minnesota football great Larry Buhler. The following year I was commissioned to create a life-size sculpture of Catherine Ford, founder of the Chambersburg Little League, near Trenton, New Jersey. After the sculpture was installed, I was commissioned to do a set of high relief sculptures of men who were also involved in the development of the same Little League program.

While living in that wonderful church in Afton, my design for the Korean War Veterans Memorial for the State of Minnesota won the commission. The project would incorporate an eight-foot-tall soldier dressed for the harsh Korean winter. Although he's in his twenties, the fatigue of war has aged him beyond his years. The soldier is walking towards an eighteen-foot-high bronze column with the silhouette of an infantryman creating a "negative space," which represents those Minnesotans still listed as missing in action. Although I get lone recognition for creating the heroic statuary to honor those who fought the "forgotten war," it was a collaborative effort with Robert Kost, a Minneapolis landscape architect at BRW. I could never have completed this memorial without Bob's vision and the untold *pro bono* hours pumped in by his team at BRW.

In the late 1990s I began receiving commissions for a variety of large-scale sculptures. In 1997, for example, a design firm in St. Paul commissioned a project for an indoor sculpture garden—complete with four life-size sculptures—for an apartment complex in Sun City, Arizona. This was followed by another project for a luxury senior residence in the town next door, Sun City West, for which I designed five life-size sculptures and the garden into which they were placed. Of course, these projects necessitated my spending a good deal of time in the Phoenix area. Being from Minnesota, I was immediately drawn to the climate and the beauty of Arizona, and subsequently settled in Carefree, Arizona, where I hope to spend the rest of my days.

Sometimes, while working on large-scale sculptures, I entertain myself with ideas for small, tabletop whimsical pieces. A radical departure from the sensuous or poetic portrayals of the human form which evoke a certain pleasure or pathos, and with which I'm most often associated, my "round" people were born to make the viewer feel good and perhaps giggle. In the art world, some have compared these images with the work of the master painter and sculptor, Botero. Despite the fact that I don't object to such a reference, I see my work as quite different, for the humor or whimsy of a piece is in the posturing of its subject. *Le Grande Danse Series* was conceived back in the seventies but was not delivered until the turn of the millennium. The world might not have been ready for such flamboyance prior to that. My *Bacchus Series* made its first appearance in 1998, followed by the debut of *The Big Band Series* in 2002. Thanks to rave reviews on both series, you can stay tuned for more whimsy in the years to come.

When people see the wide-ranging content and style of my sculpture, they sometimes express surprise at the diversity of my work. I explain to their astonishment that there are at least two reasons for the range of my work. The first is that to survive as an artist, I decided early on to accept most any commission offered to me, if appropriate both artistically and financially. I have, therefore, done portraits of family pets, national field champion dogs, and also horses. I have created sculptures showing their children playing leapfrog or holding each other close under an umbrella. The other reason, which is fortunate for me—as well as for my clients and collectors—is that I have an inquiring mind, a mind that likes to wander. The fact is that I have many interests and consider myself lucky that I can pursue more than one of these at a time. Being receptive to creating new things and having a willingness to respond to an unusual idea, I have a range of work that has been compared to Picasso, who would not be limited to any one subject or medium. Still on a journey of self-discovery, I celebrate being a creative artist who can look within and find a world of images awaiting his touch.

Untitled clay sculpture defaced and destroyed in 1984.

L E A P F R O G

*D*uring the past twenty years, I have had occasion to do more than thirty portrait sculptures. The most challenging portraits are those of children. While sitting still is the child's challenge, for the sculptor the challenge is to capture the child's essence before it changes.

Leap Frog was created at the request of Mickey and Charlie's father. Hoping I could portray their exuberance, he was most pleased—as I was—with the sculpture's feeling of flight and animation.

J E S S I C A

*I*n 1996, two life-long friends commissioned a pair of children to be cast in bronze. Up to this time, nearly all my sculptures were of the nude figure, but since Marge and Alan Larson were not interested in nude figures for their home, *Jessica* and *Tyler* are wearing swimsuits… suitable dress for their setting alongside a man-made river. Although the Larsons have several grandchildren themselves, Jessica and Tyler are my grandchildren, who were used because they were more accessible models.

TYLER

*B*oys and frogs just naturally seem to be attracted to each other. *Tyler*'s expression says he's excited about having the frog but not quite sure what to do next.

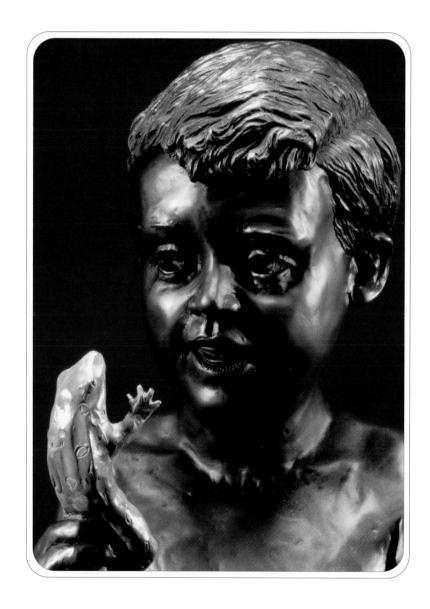

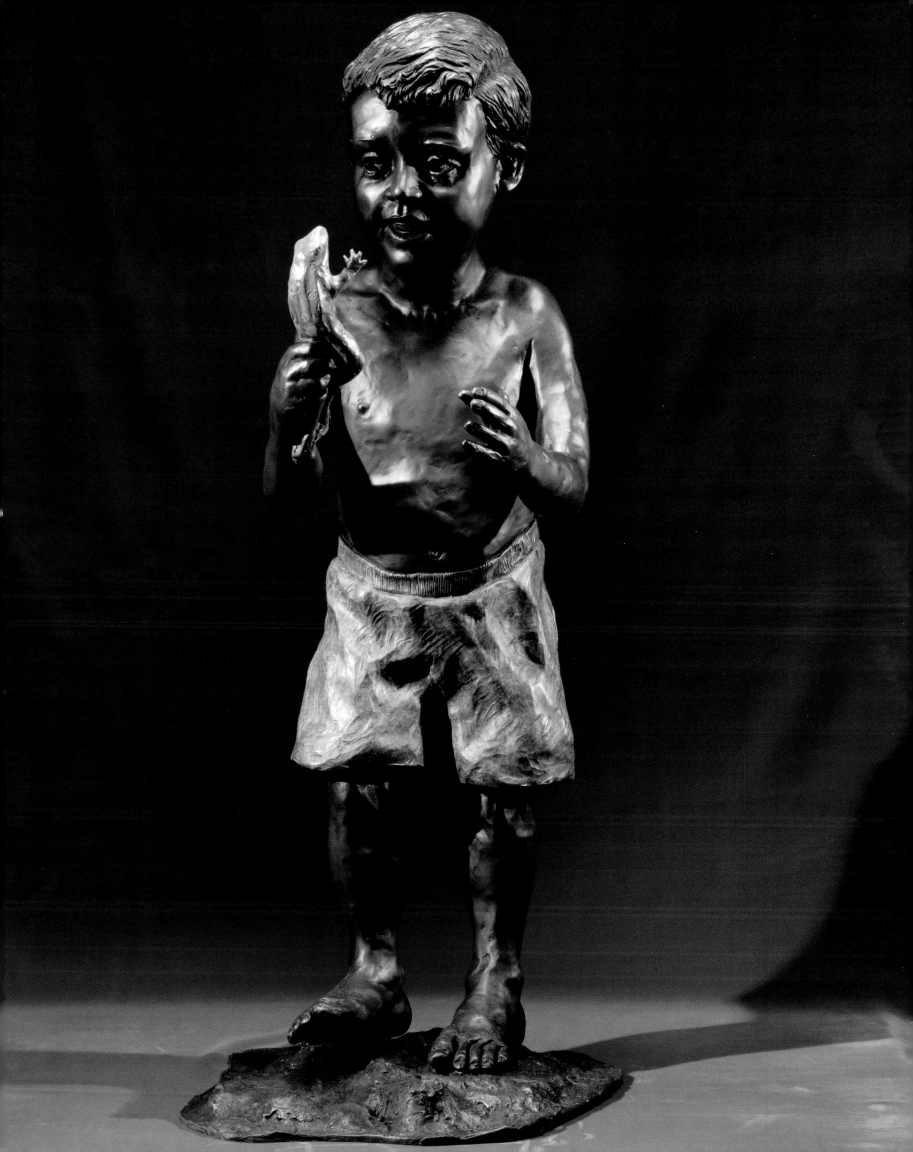

*I*n 1990–91 I created portraits of all the members of the Donn Lorenz family. The four children came to my studio in pairs, each modeling for two to three hours at a time. Having so enjoyed the artist-model dynamics in my studio, they encouraged their parents to have their portraits done as well, so the family would always be together.

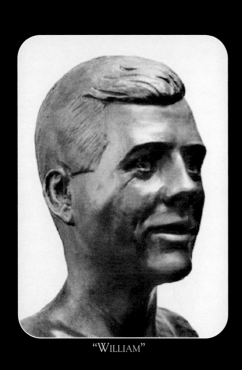

"WILLIAM"

"TINA"

"DONNA"

"KARA"

In 1999 I met Jim Venuto, an art collector from Omaha, Nebraska, who asked me to create portrait bronzes of his children. Several times over the next two years I traveled to his home with my clay models to have his children sit for an hour or two. These private sittings on the children's home turf resulted in three strong personality studies in bronze.

DEMENE

From 1988 through 1990 I had the pleasure of working with Demene Hall, a Seattle actress who performed in live theatre, movies and television, appearing a few times in a family series starring James Earl Jones. Although Demene modeled occasionally at the Pratt Art Center, this portrait was completed in my Pioneer Square studio shortly before I returned to Minnesota in 1990.

SUMMER DELIGHT

*I*magine my delight when Arizona Diamondbacks pitcher Randy Johnson asked me to create portrait sculptures of his children. What was particularly challenging for this commission was to "modify" these portraits to reflect the children as they might be several years hence. At the time, one child was four, and the other, six months. *Summer Delight*, which is situated in front of the Johnson home, is plumbed as a fountain, with the water cascading out the top of the umbrella.

$\mathcal{D}$enny Ryerson, builder and owner of the Heritage Tradition at Sun City West, commissioned me to design this collection of life-size portrait bronzes—as well as the sculpture garden itself—for the atrium of this luxury senior residence. The models included his son, Scott; my wife, Kathryn; Rebecca, the granddaughter of close friends; Lauren, the 12-year-old daughter of a business acquaintance; and finally, Chelsea, a champion dachshund.

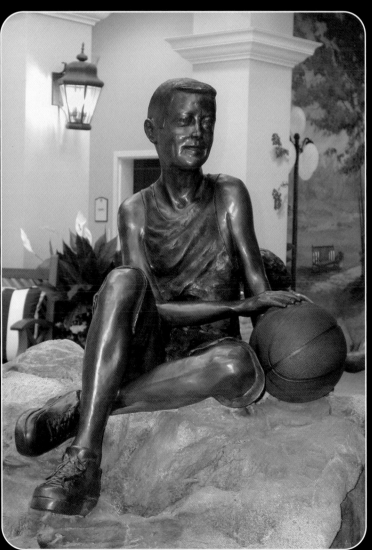

"Scott" 2002

"Lauren" 2002

"KATHRYN, REBECCA AND CHELSEA" 2002

L A N A

*I*n my work, I prefer the dynamics of working with ordinary people instead of professional models. At the opening of a group exhibit in which I participated—at a gallery in Excelsior, Minnesota—Lana walked in with her sister and mother… each one quite beautiful and elegant. I turned to my wife and said, "one of those three women will be my next model." After introducing myself and suggesting that one of them model for me, the mom and sister turned to Lana and said, "Here is your model." Lana readily agreed.

LARRY BUHLER

In 1991, my wife Kathryn and I moved to Granite Falls, Minnesota. Living in a wonderful little house on 200 feet of Minnesota River frontage, we converted a run-down auto dealership building into an art gallery and sculpture studio.

During our time in Granite Falls I received my first monumental commission to create a larger-than-life portrait of Larry Buhler, a hero of sorts to the people of Windom, Minnesota. Buhler had played football at the University of Minnesota under Bernie Bierman and went on to play in the backfield for the Green Bay Packers from 1939–41, becoming an MVP and Hall of Famer. When Buhler died, some friends suggested that a statue be made of Larry "because Windom would probably never have anyone more famous." The community was all for it, generously raising the necessary funds and commissioning the work. The eight-foot portrait of Buhler—situated on the courthouse lawn—with his football in one hand and helmet in the other is a proud reminder of a local legend.

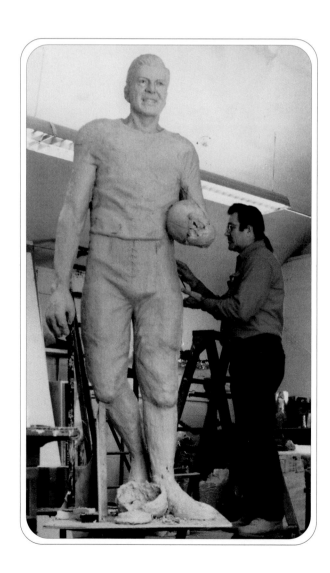

LAWRENCE "LARRY" BUHLER

1917 ⊖ 1990

WINDOM HIGH SCHOOL GRADUATE 1935

UNIVERSITY OF MINNESOTA 1935-1939

GREEN BAY PACKERS 1939-1941

VOTED

MINNESOTAS MVP

ALL AMERICAN ATHLETE 1938

GREEN BAY HALL OF FAME 1939

1942

BUSINESS FRIENDS

AMERICAN LEGION POST #206
ANDERSON-SCHMIDT
BASINGER CLINIC
BOLIN LUMBER
CALDWELL PACKING
COMMUNITY FIRST BANK
COTTONWOOD COUNTY CITIZEN
F. O. E. #3891 EAGLES CLUB
FORTUNE TRANSPORTATION
FRANK'S SHOE REPAIR
GORDY'S SUPER VALU
GREEN BAY PACKERS
HARDEE'S WINDOM
HEARTLAND STATE BANK
HIGLEY FORD SALES
HY-VEE FOOD STORE
JIM JOHNSON AGENCY
JURGENS CONSTRUCTION
KDOM RADIO
KIWANIS CLUB
KNUTH CONSTRUCTION
LAMPERT'S YARDS
MASONIC BODIES
MESSER MACHINE & MFG.

NORTHRUP KING
NORTHWEST CEDAR
PEOPLES NATURAL GAS
ED PHILLIPS AND SON
P J S LOUNGE
PIZZA BARN OF WINDOM
SCHWALBACH HARDWARE
STAPLES OIL
STEFFENS GM TOWN
SOUTHWEST STATE BANK
TASLER REAL ESTATE
WINDOM FIRE DEPARTMENT
WINDOM QUICK PRINT
WINDOM READY MIX
WINDOM SERVICEMASTER

FAMILY FRIENDS

SIG ANDERSON FAMILY
J L CALLE FAMILY
SCHWALBACH FAMILY
DOLPH STRUNK FAMILY
F W SYKORA FAMILY
J S THOMPSON FAMILY

CATHERINE FORD

*I*n 1991, I received a call from Princeton, New Jersey landscape architect Alan Goodheart, who had just redesigned a Little League park in Trenton. Residents of the Chambersburg District of Trenton had decided to honor Catherine Ford, one of the founders of the Chambersburg Little League. At the age of 80, this remarkable lady was still involved with Little League, collecting donations to support their programs and opening the concession stand during games.

After flying to New Jersey—where I met and photographed Mrs. Ford—I returned to my studio to complete her life-size portrait. Although she stood only four-foot-ten, she had an imposing presence as she collected all those nickels, dimes and quarters in a plastic cup. No wonder she got so many donations.

The following April, we returned and installed this sculpture as Chambersburg honored Catherine Ford during the Little League's opening ceremonies.

As it turned out, the people of Chambersburg had further plans for me. Upon my return to Minnesota, they commissioned me to create a set of three high relief portraits of men whose efforts were critical to the development of the Little League program in Trenton. On completion, these portraits would be permanently affixed to the Chambersburg Little League scoreboard.

ANTHONY FRASCELLA SR

MIKE CREA

AL PARROT NICOLAI

MINNESOTA KOREAN WAR VETERANS MEMORIAL

The *Korean War Veterans Memorial* was a collaborative effort between Robert Kost, a Minneapolis landscape architect at BRW, Inc., and me. When designing the memorial, Bob and I immediately agreed on several design concepts. The site was to be about people and would not have a morbid or melancholy feel, nor would it contain a granite wall. Since the dedication of the Vietnam memorial in Washington D.C., many communities had replicated that concept, but we wanted ours to be the only one of its kind.

In our design the bronze infantryman is walking in the direction of home, represented by the State Capitol building, which can be seen in the distance. The soldier is searching for his missing companion, represented by the negative space in the eighteen-foot bronze column toward which he is moving. On each end of the column there is a fifteen-foot high bas-relief showing unforgettable scenes of the Korean War while split-granite tiles inset on the walkways identify significant locations and dates.

Around the nautilus-shaped inner circle of the memorial are placed eight black granite columns separated by black granite benches; on the columns are engraved the names of those Minnesotans who are missing or whose lives were lost as a result of the Korean Conflict.

Surrounding the entire memorial are two rows of arborvitae greenery and rows of flowering trees. Beside the entry are plantings indigenous to Korea and in the sidewalk at the entrance is an eight-foot circle with a map of Korea showing the 38th parallel.

THE RESCUERS

Commissioned by the city of Peoria, Arizona in 2001, this monumental bronze stands eleven feet tall, and gives recognition to the police and fire services. It was dedicated on February 9, 2002, with several hundred people in attendance.

2001, the Sculpture in the Streets Committee of Mesa, Arizona, chose me to create four separa

be placed in Mesa. Each of these depicted a person important to the city's history: Senat

, John A. Nesbitt, Larkin Fitch, and Harvey Wood. The photos on this and the next six pages sł

rogress in my studio.

NATOR ERNEST MCFARLA

COMMISSION

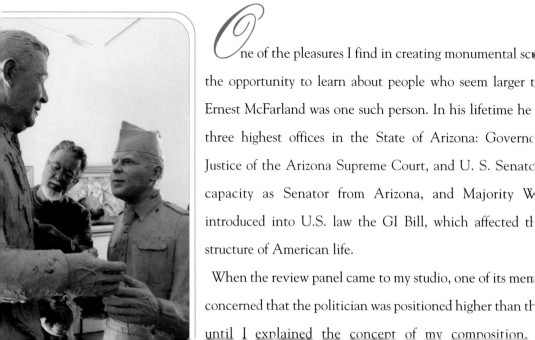

ne of the pleasures I find in creating monumental sc

the opportunity to learn about people who seem larger t

Ernest McFarland was one such person. In his lifetime he

three highest offices in the State of Arizona: Governc

Justice of the Arizona Supreme Court, and U. S. Senatc

capacity as Senator from Arizona, and Majority W

introduced into U.S. law the GI Bill, which affected tł

structure of American life.

When the review panel came to my studio, one of its mem

concerned that the politician was positioned higher than tł

until I explained the concent of my composition.

LARKIN FITCH

*I*n Arizona, pioneer families existed well into the twentieth century. After arriving here from Arkansas in 1925, Larkin Fitch became one such pioneer. Although he never received a high school diploma, he graduated from college in Tucson. As a farmer, businessman, and civic leader, Fitch made important contributions to his community, such as being instrumental in developing much of the irrigation system that still serves Arizona today and serving on the Salt River Project Board of Governors. This one-time grand master of the Masonic Lodge of the State of Arizona is well-remembered for his kinship with friends and neighbors. His generosity is best remembered by baseball fans, for Larkin Fitch donated the land for Fitch Park, the winter training home of the Chicago Cubs.

Seldom seen without a copy of the *Wall Street Journal*, Mr. Fitch is depicted—paper in hand—in this sculpture shown in progress in my studio. It was commissioned by his grandchildren and donated in 2002 to the City of Mesa, Arizona.

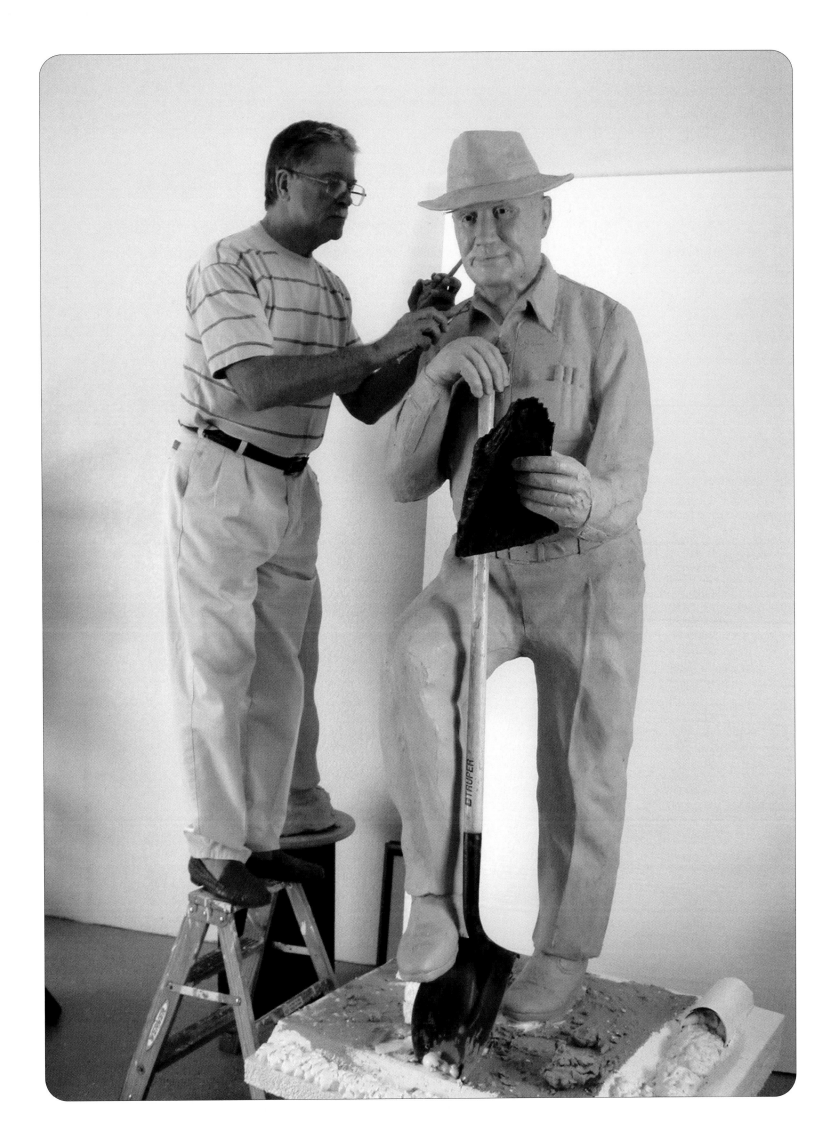

JOSEPH A. NESBITT

orn in Ireland in 1886, Joseph Nesbitt left his homeland in 1903 and made his way to Arizona in 1909. A respected residential and commercial builder, he founded a company that is now in its third generation. Among his projects was the first Masonic Lodge built in Mesa, Arizona. True to form, this life-size portrait sculpture—a gift from Nesbitt's grandchildren to the City of Mesa—will show him reviewing a set of blueprints. The studio photo shows the clay model being approved by his son and daughter-in-law, Tom and Ruth Nesbitt.

HARVEY WOOD

*T*his sculpture was donated to the city of Mesa by the family of Harvey Wood, to honor the third generation citrus farmer, as well as his fellow citrus farmers. In the likeness of Wood, the sculpture shows a citrus farmer sitting on an orange crate, peeling a naval orange for his daughter… using his signature method of how an orange was to be peeled.

EARL B. OLSON

This retired businessman and philanthropist from rural Minnesota provided a sizeable gift to help build the YMCA for the community of Willmar, Minnesota. I was commissioned by the YMCA board to create this portrait of Mr. Olson, to be cast in bronze and placed at the site of the new YMCA building.

MARIE, B.C.

While using the drawing studio at the Pratt Fine Art Center in Seattle, I created many clay figure studies following the same time routine used by my studio companions who were working with charcoal or pen and ink. The result was a collection of very spontaneous clay sketches and an increased ability to rapidly interpret what I was seeing.

The best of these clay sketches is *Marie, B.C.* The title refers to the very primitive modeling that defines form, but not detail. The model was an eighty year-old woman named Marie who presented us with her beautifully rounded and very feminine body. The clay sketch was completed in approximately twenty minutes.

L E A H

Leah was a studio study from my time at Seattle's Pratt Fine Art Center. Working with water-based clay I worked spontaneously, watching Leah move through her poses for all the drawing students. Although *Leah* appears to be lost in thought there is an almost palpable tension in her pose as a result of the frequent pose changes she was required to make during the studio session.

E S H A N

I like the introspective quality of this sculpture. *Eshan* was created as a series of demonstrations for a sculpture class that I taught in Monroe, Washington. The sculpture is finely modeled… as was the model himself.

A M Y

When I returned to Minnesota in 1990, I was introduced to a new collector and patron. His first commission was a half life-size nude, entitled *Elizabeth*. Following my completion of *Elizabeth*, he asked me to search out a model for a life-size bronze nude. I was told that in a rural community of eighteen-thousand it might be impossible to find a good looking young woman who would be willing to model nude. As it turned out, my youngest daughter encouraged her friend, Amy, to step up to the plate. At twenty-three, Amy—an accomplished swimmer and tennis player—was the picture perfect model for my first life-size nude sculpture.

This sculpture created quite a stir when a school tour of fifth-grade students saw it in my Granite Falls gallery! Much to my surprise and delight, however, Amy's parents—on seeing the sculpture—congratulated me on creating such a fine likeness of their daughter.

Sadly, the molds to *Amy* were lost in 1998 when we lost our home in Afton, Minnesota to fire. *The Blue Nude* torso, pictured opposite, is a partial casting of *Amy* that I have always found pleasing.

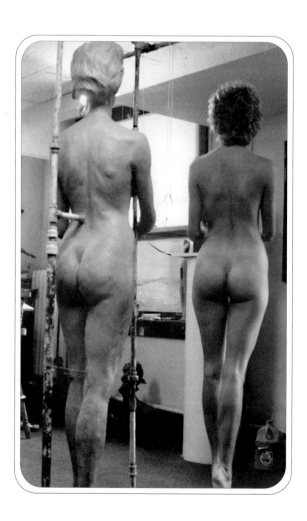

THE WALKOVER

"*S*eldom is the beauty, grace and strength of a young woman shown with such clarity as a young gymnast at the apex of her walkover on the balance beam."

The Walkover was my first life-size sculpture. Having lost the commission because there were no panty lines on the leotard, I borrowed money to cast this sculpture, which was purchased years later by a collector in Seattle.

HOMAGE

Homage is another life-drawing studio sculpture. It was originally created in terra cotta, which allowed me to work very rapidly. This sculpture captures the physical strength, beauty and grace of the model who had a tremendous presence in spite of being barely five feet tall.

I believe sculptors should spend time making studio studies in clay, using the same time format that is used to teach painters to create their images in just a few minutes. The resulting spontaneity develops the sculptor's reflexes and confidence, while giving rise to a very natural, albeit primitive, piece of art.

Le Grande Danse Series...
PETITE DANCE FIGURES – GISELLE, SERGEI, ANTICIPATION, THE LIFT

This whimsical collection of dancers began strictly as self-entertainment. The response was so great that I cast all but one of the images in bronze. These were the inspiration for all the whimsical works to follow.

I am frequently asked of my motivation to create "fat" sculpture, which my wife refers to as "overly Rubenesque." The truth is that I no longer see these figures as fat, but as great round sculpture elements. I have actually been fascinated by this form since the late seventies, when I began engraving rubenesque figures in ivory (scrimshaw).

NICK AND NORA

*M*y mind has time to wander as I go through the process of creating new sculpture. As *Nick and Nora* developed into a cohesive concept, I came to see the couple as quite sophisticated, from a time more elegant than ours. For Nora, I created a new gown trimmed at the bottom with a frothy fabric, giving way to a high slit on the side to allow her freedom of movement.

Nick could only be a gentleman of Central or South America—a General—as so many of those gentlemen are. His tuxedo flies as the couple tangos through the night, his epaulets and medals flashing in the starlight.

E U R O P A

*T*he figures of my *Grande Danse Series* are meant to show the joy of life, free of inhibition. *Europa*, in the final analysis, is also a spoof on the tall, slinky sculptures of Erte. Most striking, however, is her unfettered freedom to just be herself.

Some collectors believe that *Europa* is not only a member of the *Grande Danse* series, but also an extension of the *Bacchus* series with her apparent affinity for grapes and merriment.

THE LIFT

*T*he original "petite" version of *The Lift* was such a success and such a joy that I could not help but create this larger version. I frequently joke that this sculpture might also be entitled "*Optimism*" for very obvious reasons.

ANTONIO

When I think of free spirits I cannot help but think of Anthony Quinn and the character he portrayed in *Zorba the Greek*. I suspect he was a free spirit in real life as well. Although this sculpture was not created in Anthony Quinn's likeness, I cannot deny that Zorba's persona was in my mind as I created it.

THE THIRD ARABESQUE

*T*his title came to me when a young couple, who were ballet dancers, saw the sculpture. She hugged her partner and screamed, "Look, it's the third arabesque!" Some time later, a conservative-looking woman—when she heard me mention the title—responded, "Oh, no. The third arabesque is more like this" and struck a very elegant dance pose. I responded, "My dear, she is doing the best she can!"

LADY GODIVA

The winter of 1990, when I returned to Minnesota from Seattle, was particularly cold and snowy, causing me to spend an inordinate amount of time eating! Perhaps as a result of that winter's food-focused existence, I created three very rotund horses and an even more rotund rhinoceros. A corpulent *Lady G* was actually an afterthought intended to provide some balance to the weighty compositions.

NORA

*I*n the whimsical dance series, *Nora* was the first woman to wear a full gown, which I designed to carry out the Tango theme and to suit her proportions. I love the presentation of this round figure in her elegant gown, seemingly floating on air. Forever light on her feet, *Nora* was cast as an individual sculpture for the first time in 2001.

THUMBELINA

Thumbelina is one of my most successful whimsical bronzes. She was created while we lived in Afton, Minnesota and was half life-size vertically, but life-size horizontally!

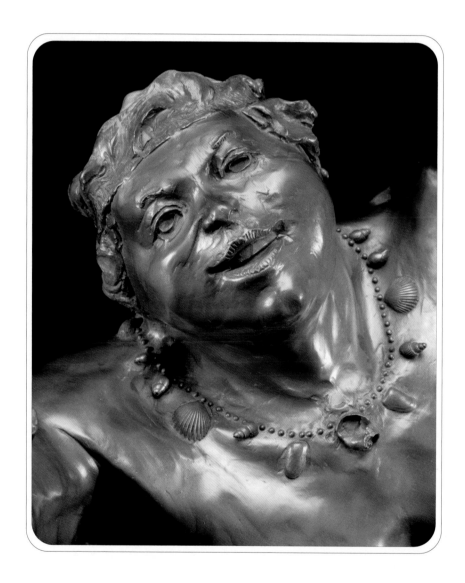

BACCHUS & CYBIL

In 1990 I spent a week in Paris with my son, Kevin, who is a landscape architect. We spent our time touring gardens, parks and museums around Paris. It was in one of those gardens that I found a large terra cotta sculpture of Bacchus on a burro, surrounded by dancing girls. At the end of the day I discovered the film had not loaded properly and my photo of Bacchus was fixed only in my memory! When I returned home I was determined to create a sculpture as playful, and in 2000 I cast both a small and large version of Bacchus, the Greek God of wine and merriment!

According to legend, there was a sect of women called Cybils who were seers and sorceresses. Greek mythology tells us that Cybil was caught up in the lustier side of life. What a perfect companion she would be to Bacchus! I named their trusted steed (hog) Harley, as a tongue-in-cheek reference to the celebrated motorcycle.

The petite version of *Bacchus & Cybil* is one of the very best examples of what I like my sculptures to be. It is based on two figures from Greek mythology, but the addition of the pig carries it to a new level of whimsy.

JOAN OF ART –
ATTACKING HER WORK WITH VIGOR!

*J*oan of Art was created as a companion to my petite *Bacchus & Cybil*. Initially, I considered creating the girl as Joan of Arc from French history, but since none of my sculpture reflects war or conflict I felt it inappropriate. Thus *Joan of Art*, my not-so-starving artist. Instead of arrows, her quiver contains paintbrushes… those being her weapons of choice. The pallet is dabbed with splotches of paint.

Always enjoying a play on words, I named Joan's pig, *Vigor*, the resulting title that titters with its double entendre.

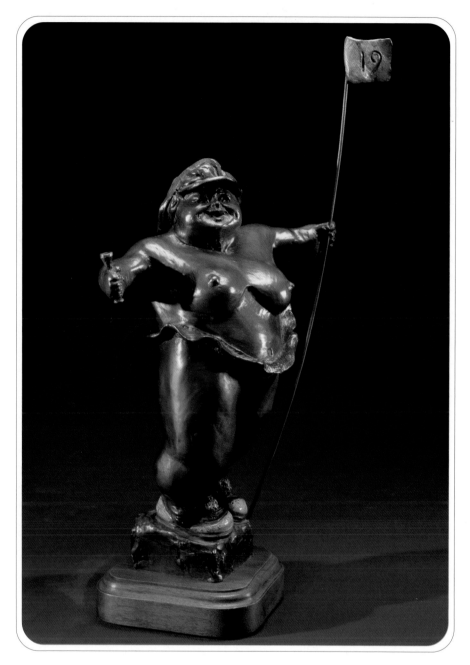

BARBIE

*T*o veteran golfers, golf and Arizona are synonymous. Living on Arizona turf, I recognized that it was important to have some golfers among my sculptures, or pay the penalty! The most charming of these is, perhaps, *Barbie*. Since many courses require golfers to wear a collar to meet the dress code—and since *Barbie* does not meet it for obvious reasons—she waits, clubless, at the 19th hole!

THREE AMIGOS

*H*andicap aside, these golfers are gems in the rough. Retired, they've got plenty of time to get a grip and go the distance.

THE WATER HAZARD   READING THE BREAK   THE LONG DRIVE

Reaffirming my *joie de vivre*, my joy-of-life attitude, in my own life and work, I couldn't pass up the opportunity to create *The Big Band Series*. From the very start of this series, each musical maestro was an immediate hit with my collectors. Beyond their up-beat celebrity distinction, their physical presence gives new meaning to "big band."

*S*ometimes an old idea comes forth and causes the development of a new sculpture. A unique terra cotta sculpture dating back to China's Seventh Century Tang Dynasty provided the concept and model for this set of bronzes. Although they are based on the antique clay, I have given them a more contemporary interpretation. The green marble and cherry base gives them an Asian elegance.

THE EMPRESS

*T*he *Empress* is a twenty-four inch bronze depicting elaborate livery and one rear leg lifted.

ROSEBUD

Rosebud shows more animation and movement, with one front foot raised and decorated with elaborate livery.

FOUR SQUARE

Among the many variations seen in the horses of the Tang Dynasty, this simple presentation known as the "four square" is the most prevalent. Four Square is the classic pose with all four feet squarely positioned.

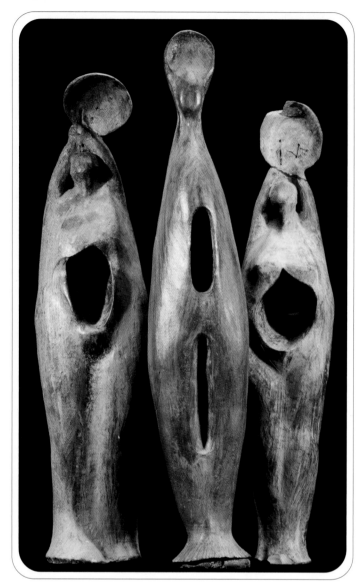

The *Native Women Series* was a concept which needed time to germinate before the idea became a fully developed sculpture. In 1989, my son, Kevin, a landscape architect in Eden Prairie, Minnesota, introduced me to a prospective client with an interest in a large-scale outdoor sculpture. What she described was a sculpture which would be abstract, feminine, Native American (preferably Chippewa), but would not interfere with her view of the lake. The design I proposed was the *Rice Basket*, an eight-foot sculpture based on the three maquettes shown here. Although I ultimately did not get the commission, I kept these maquettes for twelve years before creating the *Rice Basket*, which was the first in my *Native Women Series*. Each figure in the series is simply presented and provides an unpretentious and loving look at beautiful women of all cultures.

RICE BASKET

The *Rice Basket* and subsequent native women exemplify the inner strength and beauty of the mature woman. The curve and density of the full, mature female figure lends itself to great sculptural form.

A simple turquoise necklace and earrings accent the simplicity of the dress, and direct the eye to the poignant expression of contentment and passion on her face.

A M A ' S   G I F T

There is a dual meaning in this title. First, *Ama's* (American Indian word for grandmother's) gift was in giving life to her children, and then the lifelong gifts of love and sustenance.

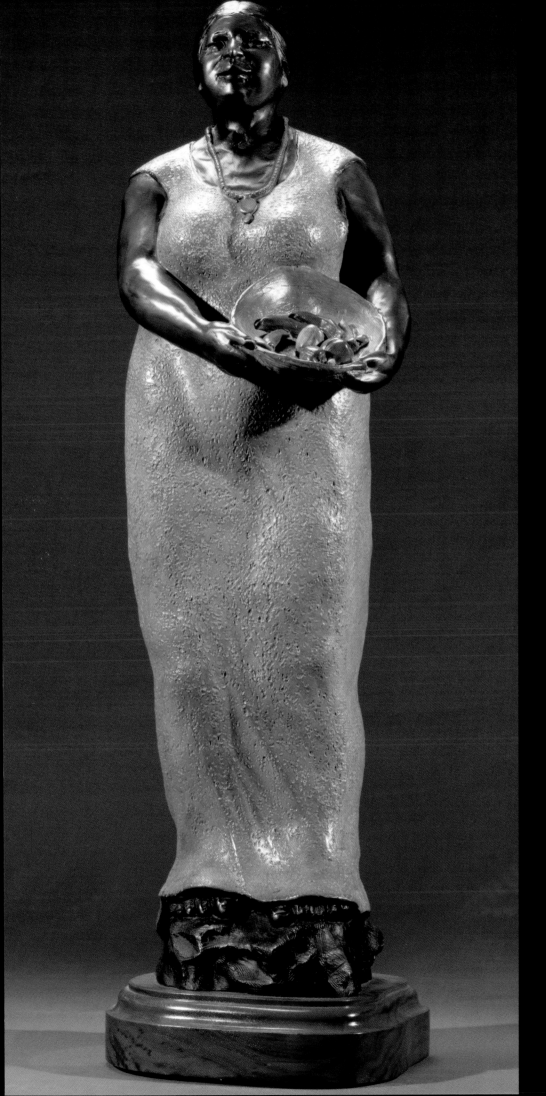

CHILI PEPPERS

*N*ot only is this woman statuesque, I think the expression on her face seems to say that she is no shrinking violet, but one hot pepper!

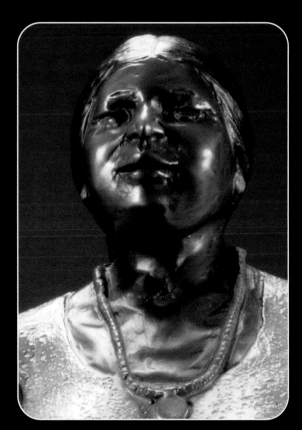

WATERCARRIER

*T*his elegant tabletop sculpture has an almost larger-than-life presence. I think the simple lines and full-bodied mature figure make a strong statement of what good sculpture is about.

Shaman Series...

$\mathcal{E}$ach of my Shaman is based on the simple triangular wedge. Just as the hourglass represents the female figure, this wedge embodies the simple masculine build, which is wide at the shoulders and tapers through the figure to his feet. I have modified the lateral view by emphasizing the Shaman's shoulder curve and buttocks to amplify the first impression that this is a "man masquerading as an animal." As your eye drops to the bottom of the figure, however, the contour of the robe does not accurately follow the curve of the man's leg. Only when you continue to turn the sculpture do you learn that this "man" has the feet of a four-legged animal. The Elk, the Bison, the Moose … where does reality separate from fantasy? Is this man masquerading as animal or is this an animal in the guise of a man? Or is the reality that one is becoming the other?

W A P I T I   S P I R I T

$\mathcal{E}$very culture expresses its spirituality in its own way. Stories become legend… myth… religion, and are then visited from a different perspective when we, as outsiders, look in. So it is with the Shaman. I have looked through windows at the spirituality of the American Indian and made my interpretations. Slightly surreal, the Shaman—*Wapiti Spirit*—is spreading his hands benevolently, bringing protection to believers. The coup stick with the symbolic eagle feathers, medicine bag, bird-wing whistle and bear claws represent the collected power of this Shaman.

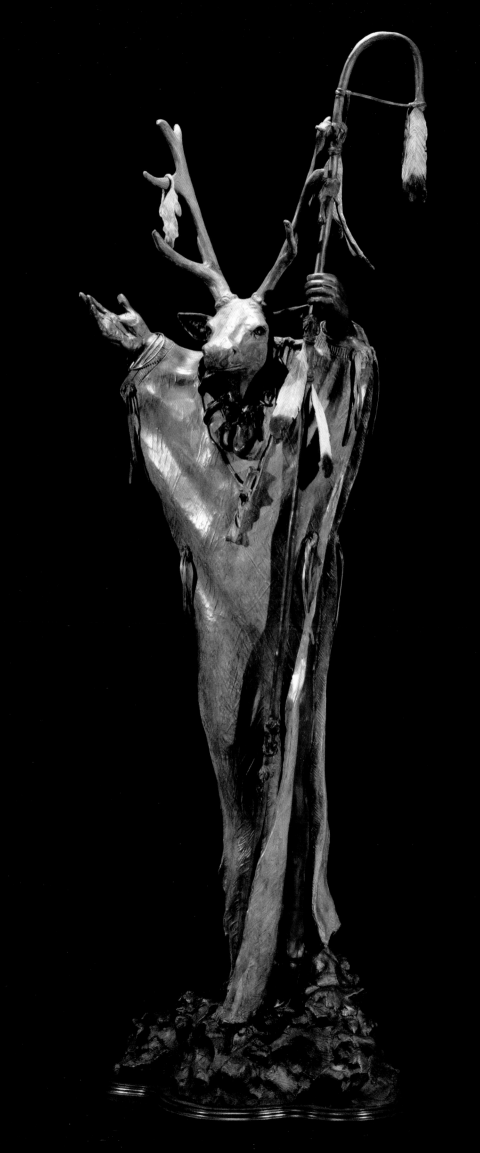

TWO FEATHERS

I don't always get it right the first time! *Two Feathers* was originally a nude, meant to be a tabletop companion to *Lana*. I kept the clay model in my studio to study for a few weeks before casting, and found I was bored by it after several days, so I set out to change it. I had been developing the leather-look of my Shaman at that time and decided to clothe this sculpture in remnants of leather. The result was this much more interesting figure.

Art working on the clay model for Two Feathers.

BUFFALO FETISH

I created this great little fetish in 2002 as a companion to the larger *Fetish Bear*.

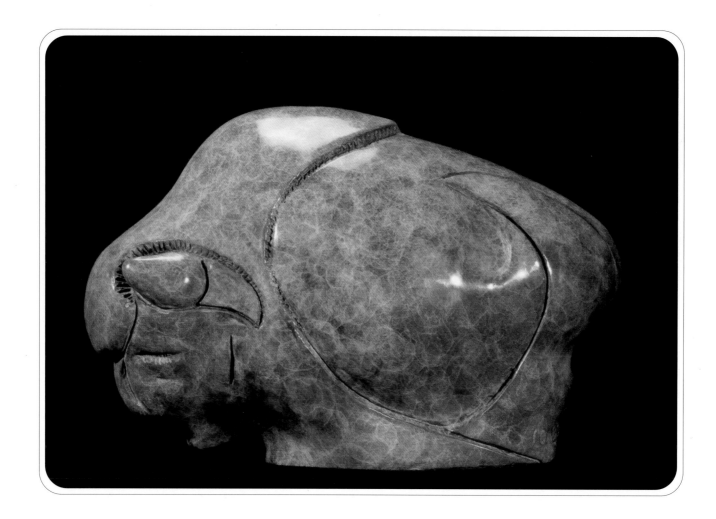

FETISH BEAR

T his bronze, opposite, was created shortly after I returned to Minnesota from Seattle in 1990. I was still influenced by the Seattle pastels and the large sweeping curves of the drawings I made in the late eighties. The clean simple form of the bear is accented by incised lines, or scores, and inverted curves. Although I have used other patinas, the white watermark patina is the most striking.

JONETTE'S HORSE

This is the second sculpture I produced in 1982. I began the sculpture about 10:00 p.m. one night when I was angry with the world. By 2:00 a.m., my mood had mellowed and I went to bed. Although my frame of mind had changed, the horse continued to be wild and free. I placed a feather in its tail to indicate that this wild creature had not always known this freedom. Over the years, several collectors have asked if this sculpture was somewhat autobiographical.

Jonette's Horse was produced in an edition of ten castings. I also produced two other sculptures based on this wild creature.

PRAIRIE SISTER

*P*rairie Sister refers to the sister cities of Willmar, Minnesota and Frameries, Belgium. This sculpture was created in 1990 as a gift to the city of Frameries from the city of Willmar. The sculpture was modeled in a pasture where two young Belgian mares were turned out for me to use as models. I left the feet hidden in the base to represent the heavy draft horses walking through soft earth. At that time, I used a traditional black patina, but have since given it a new, more contemporary patina.

WINDY RIDGE

*S*ome poses seem almost classic in their simplicity and that is how I feel about *Windy Ridge*. Holding her ground on a windy hillside, ears back and eyes closed, the horse stands with her back to the wind, her mane and tail blustering forward. One can almost feel the snow that is soon to come.

WINDY RIDGE

Though I usually try to present my sculpture in compact and graceful poses, this bronze has no compactness. *Last Tango* shows the cowboy parting company with his horse after it slips on icy ground and breaks the cinch holding the saddle safely in place. The sudden release of the rider prompts his expression of hope for safer ground.

PARTING COMPANY
Arthur H. Norby

In 1982, I was so wrapped up in operating two art galleries that I only produced two sculptures. In creating *On a Cold Trail Home* I tried to capture the disgruntled mood of the horse and the bone-chilling cold of the rider as they moved across the hard wet ground. I based this scene on the many rides I'd taken between 1972 and 1979, when my family and I raised horses and cattle on a 40-acre farmsite near Willmar, Minnesota.

I was inspired to create this sculpture by the man who commissioned it. Bill Eaton, a successful hotelier who, at the age of seventeen, rode this bull during the Pendelton, Oregon Round Up. Although the bull ride took place in 1941, Bill's memories of the ride are still vivid today.

I placed all the weight of this sculpture on the bull's hind feet, with its front feet raised and a distinct twist in its strong body. The rider is completely airborne, showing the remarkable power of the bull. This was not a dance one would likely forget.

*I*nitially I titled this sculpture *Hombre* because of his "total cowboy" attitude, but later began calling it

Tombstone.

This sculpture was commissioned by Maurice Turner in 1991 and completed in 1992. Although he did not

actually model for the sculpture, I created it in his image. Mr. Turner had previously commissioned an angel for

his mother's grave marker, and indicated this sculpture would be on the mantle in his home until his own

demise, and would then be placed on his tombstone… hence the new title!